LAND BUYING CHECKLIST

RALPH M. LEWIS

FOURTH EDITION

Home Builder Press®
National Association of Home Builders

This publication is designed to provide accurate and authoritative information in regard to the subject matter covered. It is sold with the understanding that neither the author nor the publisher is engaged in rendering legal, accounting, or other professional service. If legal advice or other expert assistance is required, the services of a competent professional person should be sought.

—From a Declaration of Principles jointly adopted by a Committee of the American Bar Association and a Committee of Publishers and Associations.

Land Buying Checklist

ISBN: O-86718-358-6

© 1981, 1985, 1988, 1990 by Home Builder Press® of the National Association of Home Builders

All rights reserved. No part of this book may be reproduced or utilized in any form or by any means, electronic or mechanical, including photocopying and recording, or by an information storage and retrieval system without permission in writing from the publisher.

Printed in the United States of America

For further information, please contact:
    Home Builder Bookstore
    National Association of Home Builders
    15th and M Streets, N.W.
    Washington, D.C. 20005
    (800) 368-5242

12/90 ATLIS/AUTOMATED 4K

Introduction

The *Land Buying Checklist* provides an effective means of evaluating all the critical factors affecting the suitability of a piece of land for purchase and development. The items in this checklist are based on the experiences of both our own company and many of our colleagues in the housing industry.

In this fourth edition, we have made numerous changes based on our experiences, including consolidating some of the sections, adding a summary form noting the problematic aspects of the property, and various items concerning environmental aspects of the site (toxics, hazardous wastes, endangered species, and wetlands), and we have expanded the section pertaining to entitlements to take into account the ever increasing complexities.

Anyone who has bought land only to find out later that it has problems that are costly or impossible to solve, knows the disappointment that follows. We hope this checklist will prevent builders from making the kinds of costly errors that occur when land has not been examined adequately before purchase.

> Ralph M. Lewis
> Chairman of the Board
> Lewis Homes Group of Companies

About the Author

Ralph M. Lewis serves as chairman of the board of the Lewis Homes Group of Companies. Since founding the company in 1957, Ralph has overseen the construction of 40,000 single-family homes and 8,000 apartments, as well as numerous commercial and industrial projects. He is a life director of the National Association of Home Builders, a life director and past president of the Building Industry Association of Southern California, and a speaker at NAHB conventions and Pacific Coast Builders conferences. As an attorney, a certified public accountant, a general building contractor, and a real estate broker, Ralph has taught classes in real estate, finance, accounting, and taxation at the University of Southern California, the University of California at Los Angeles, and Los Angeles City College. Ralph has recently been appointed as the University of Southern California's first "Developer in Residence" for the Lusk Center for Real Estate Development, and counsels faculty and students.

Ralph and his wife, Goldy, were named "Builder of the Year" in 1987 by *Professional Builder* magazine. In addition, Ralph has been inducted into the National Housing Center's Hall of Fame. In 1990, Ralph and Goldy were named Persons of the Year by the National Housing Conference.

Acknowledgments

The author gratefully acknowledges the assistance of Ruth Factor, associate counsel of Lewis Homes Management Corp., Donald M. Thompson, CPA and Director of Corporate Affairs, and all of the other employees—among them, our land buyers, project managers, and financial analysts—who took time to critically review the *Checklist* and suggest additions and improvements for this edition. A special thanks to Gretchen K. Gerber, whose skills on the word processor were essential to the preparation of the manuscript.

This book was produced under the general direction of Kent Colton, NAHB Executive Vice President, in association with NAHB staff members James E. Johnson, Jr., Staff Vice President, Operations and Information Services; Adrienne Ash, Assistant Staff Vice President, Publishing Services; Rosanne O'Connor, Director of Publications; Mary E. Cox, Publications Editor; and David Rhodes, Art Director.

Table of Contents

How to Use the Land Buying Checklist
1. Preparer's Comments and Conclusions 1
2. Summary/Routing Schedule 3
3. Purchase Summary 5
4. Purchase Agreement Data 7
5. Condition of Title 13
6. Physical Aspects 17
7. Utility Availability 29
8. Entitlements 35
9. Development Costs 43
10. Market Area and Proposed Product 47
11. Financial Projections 55
12. Resale 57
13. Post-Closing Checklist 59

How to Use the Land Buying Checklist

- This Checklist should be filled out as completely as possible. Ideally you should start your investigation prior to making an offer on land; more likely, you will begin after the opening of escrow. The results of your investigation typically have a bearing on the commitment of capital funds. The initial feasibility study may be performed quickly, mostly by telephone. During the escrow period, the *Checklist* should be refined with more precise answers. The subdivision costs should be revised and refined, as they become available. The *Checklist* should be completed before any deposits "go hard" and must be completed before closing escrow.
- This checklist is intended as a workbook. All information and notes should be put directly onto the *Checklist* rather than on separate pieces of paper. Write neatly. Avoid copying from one set of notes to another so that unintentional alterations will not occur.
- Use pencil, not ink, so that you can correct answers when you obtain better information.
- Wherever possible, indicate sources of information, such as "per John Smith, City Engineer," and date obtained.
- Read and respond to every line. In cases where the question is clearly not applicable, write "N/A." It is recommended that you fill out a new *Checklist* when you are examining a parcel of land adjacent to land you have previously checked and developed.
- Whenever a question requires an answer that needs to be expanded or explained, write the answer in the space provided for "Additional Notes" at the end of each section. For example, if the answer to the question "any other existing trust deed liens?" is "yes," a full description should be given.
- Various people or departments (as reflected on the routing schedule) may be involved in completing portions of the *Checklist,* although any one person could do the whole job. Ideally, one individual should compile the replies of other individuals so that one master document is used as the source upon which you will rely. That same individual should draft the "Preparer's Comments and Conclusions Regarding Special Problems/Strengths" in order to highlight any aspects of the transaction which are problematic, high-risk, or make the particular parcel of land desirable. With respect to problems and high risks, the preparer should also discuss mitigation measures and the cost of such mitigation. A page entitled "Notes" is provided for similar comments by experts in the various departments and

by top management. This checklist should be presented to the decision makers accompanied by relevant reports, studies, and computer generated financial information.

- Because many people in a large company may need to know of the purchase while only one *Checklist* is being completed, the two summary forms should be completed and copies routed to those who need to know of the transaction (the Purchase Summary, when escrow is opened, and the Post-Closing Checklist, when the purchase has been completed).

- Be sure to give meaningful answers. If questions are taken lightly or skipped over, a costly problem may arise later. Do not assume (for example, that an easement can be quit-claimed). If a clear answer is not possible, explain the problem, rather than give an erroneous answer.

- This checklist is actually a list of mistakes, either mistakes the author has made himself, or ones he has seen others make. In the past, substantial losses have occurred because someone forgot to check something. The final decision to buy or not buy land is based on the answers in this checklist. A careless answer can easily result in costly mistakes. As mistakes have been detected, the hard way, appropriate items have been added to the *Checklist*. Given the unique aspects of every land transaction and the changing times, the user should continually be alert for problems not covered in this book, and add additional items to the *Checklist* that are the result of his or her own experience, and of local conditions.

Notes

Department

Engineering
  By _____

Marketing
  By _____

Design
  By _____

Construction
  By _____

Legal
  By _____

Financial/
  Treasurer
  By _____

Tax
  By _____

Regional
Manager's
Notes

CEO's
Notes

Preparer's Comments and Conclusions Regarding Special Problems/Strengths

For all negative aspects of the site or transaction: (1) describe the problem; (2) summarize how it could be resolved; and (3) explain its impact on the overall feasibility of the development. Also, if there are especially positive aspects of the site or transaction, explain them in the space below.

Purchase Agreement Data:

Condition of Title:

Physical Aspects:

Utility Availability:

Entitlements:

Development Costs:

Market Area and Proposed Product:

Resale:

2

Summary/Routing Schedule

Central File Name of Land: _____

Land description _____ acres; _____ possible/actual lots; at _____

_____ in _____ , _____ .

Asking Price: $ _____ acre/lot; $ _____ total.

Our proposed use: _____

Entitlements: Present status (map, zoning, general plan amendment, etc.): _____

_____ .

Goal: Tentative Tract Map approval by _____

Key dates	Target date	Date done
Title review period ends	_____	_____
Project strategy (kickoff) meeting	_____	_____
Feasibility period ends	_____	_____
Pre-submittal meeting	_____	_____
Deposit(s) released	_____	_____
Planning Commission hearing/TTM OK	_____	_____
Close escrow by	_____	_____

Checklist Completion Schedule:

	Due by	Completed by (Initials/Date)	Open items
Legal	_____	_____	_____
Engineering	_____	_____	_____
Marketing	_____	_____	_____
Financial (Pro forma)	_____	_____	_____
Regional Manager/C.E.O.	_____	_____	_____
Return to Legal (_____) to close	_____	_____	_____

Owner: _____ Phone _____

Address _____

Owner's attorney/agent _____ Phone _____

Escrow Co. _____ Phone _____
Title Co. _____ Phone _____
Consultants: Engineer _____ Phone _____
              Soils _____ Phone _____
              Toxics _____ Phone _____
              Biological _____ Phone _____
              Other _____ Phone _____
                    _____ Phone _____
                    _____ Phone _____

3

Purchase Summary

Compiled by: _____ Date: _____

Seller: _____

Buyer: _____

Location: _____

A. Transaction Summary

    1. Opening of escrow: _____

    2. Free look period: _____

        Comments: _____
        _____
        _____

    3. Title review period: _____

    4. Other contingency period(s): _____
        _____
        _____
        _____

    5. Closing date: _____

    6. Conditions precedent to closing: _____
        _____
        _____

B. Financial Summary

    1. Deposit amount: $ _____

        Paid by: _____

        Release date: _____

        Security for release: _____

    2. Additional deposit: $ _____

        Due: _____

        Paid by: _____

        Release date: _____

        Security for release: _____

    3. Liquidated damages: $ _____

4. Cash at close: $ _____

5. New/assumed note at close: $ _____

   _____ Interest rate: _____ %

   _____ Payments: _____

   _____ Due date: _____

   _____ Releases: _____

6. Tax considerations reviewed? _____

   Comments: _____
   _____

4

Purchase Agreement Data

Compiled by: _____ Date: _____

1. a. Owner/Seller: _____
   b. Who are the principals/partners of owner? _____
   c. Do you anticipate any dissident joint owners who may delay or kill the sale? _____
   d. Special information concerning owner: _____
   _____
   e. If owner is public agency, what is procedure for sale? _____
   _____

2. How are we planning to take title (name of entity and/or joint venture partner)? _____

3. If this is a "flip deal" (i.e. seller is in escrow to purchase the site he or she is offering to us):
   a. List the key terms of the underlying transaction: _____
   _____
   b. What are the onerous terms (if any)? _____
   _____
   c. Have we received and reviewed the documents for the underlying transaction? _____

4. a. Name any third party who may assert an interest in the site by virtue of any recently expired purchase and sale agreement or option to purchase: _____
   b. Has this party agreed to quit-claim his/her/its interest in the site? _____

5. List any easements or rights-of-way owner has given or been granted in connection with the site which are not of record (include easements promised by or to owner but not yet granted): _____
   _____

6. a. Does owner want to control how we develop or what we put on the land? _____
   b. Do we have access to land prior to close of escrow? _____
   c. Are there any other limitations on our activities prior to or after close of escrow? _____
   _____
   d. Is owner retaining any portion of the land? _____
   e. If land has not been surveyed, will owner bear or share cost of survey? _____

7. a. Which party is paying for the environmental assessment? _____

b. Is owner providing certification from state-registered engineer or certified engineering geologist, based on inspection of land and records, that no evidence exists of contamination by hazardous or toxic materials? _____

c. Is owner providing notarized statement attesting to nonexistence of problems relating to hazardous or toxic contamination of land? _____

d. Is owner agreeing to indemnify for any future liability resulting from hazardous or toxic contamination of land? _____

e. Does owner have financial strength to make indemnity good? _____

f. Will owner issue "comfort letter" regarding electric or magnetic radiation field health risk? _____

8. Property Tax Assessor's parcel number: _____

9. a. Any physical improvements? _____

    b. Approximate value: _____

    c. Describe condition: _____

    d. Will any physical improvements or existing structures have to be demolished? _____

    e. Can they be demolished without violating a no-waste clause in the existing trust deed? _____

10. a. Any refunds (infrastructure, or otherwise) due to seller which are assigned to us? _____

    b. How much? _____

    c. When are they due? _____

11. a. Any income produced by land? _____

    b. If land is leased, what are the terms? _____

    c. How much notice is required to terminate lease? _____

12. Amount and kind of insurance carried: _____

13. Source of lead to land: _____

14. a. Real estate broker/salesperson: _____

    Address: _____

    Phone: _____

    b. 1. Percent commission: _____

        2. Will broker cooperate on commission? _____

        3. Who pays broker's commission? _____

        4. Can payment of commission be deferred? _____

    c. 1. Type of listing: _____

        2. Have we seen the listing? _____

15. Price and terms:
    a. Price: per acre $_____ per lot $_____ per front foot $_____
    b. Total price $_____
    c. Cash down payment and terms: _____
       _____

       Release for down payment? _____
    d. If stock of corporate owner is to be acquired, will seller agree to corporate audit and retain all liabilities from prior corporate operations? _____

16. New purchase money trust deed ☐ or contract for deed ☐:
    a. Principal amount of indebtedness $_____
    b. 1. Payments made to: _____
       2. How often? _____
    c. Amount of each installment $_____
    d. Interest at rate of: _____
    e. How is interest paid? _____
    f. Any balloon payments required in future? _____
    g. Can this instrument be assumed by a subsequent buyer? _____
    h. Can balance be prepaid without penalty at any time? _____
    i. Can this trust deed be subordinated to construction loans? _____
    j. Can portions of land be released without full payment? _____
    k. Is there a no-waste clause in the trust deed or other pertinent document? _____
    l. Can we substitute security if payments are restricted? _____
    m. Does trust deed preclude personal liability or deficiency judgment? _____
    n. Is trustee under trust deed acceptable to us? _____
    o. Is there an acceleration clause in the note or trust deed? _____
    p. Are there any other provisions we want stricken or modified? _____
       _____

17. Assumable existing purchase money trust deed ☐:
    a. Principal amount of indebtedness $_____
    b. 1. Payments made to: _____
       2. How often? _____
    c. Amount of each installment $_____
    d. Interest at rate of: _____
    e. How is interest paid? _____

f. Any balloon payments required in future? _____

g. Can this instrument be assumed by a subsequent buyer? _____

h. Can balance be prepaid without penalty at any time? _____

i. Can this trust deed be subordinated to construction loans? _____

j. Can portions of land be released without full payment? _____

k. Is there a no-waste clause in the trust deed or other pertinent document? _____

l. Can we substitute security if payments are restricted? _____

m. Does trust deed preclude personal liability or deficiency judgment? _____

n. Is trustee under trust deed acceptable to us? _____

o. Is there an acceleration clause in the existing note or trust deed? _____

p. Are there any other provisions we want stricken or modified? _____
_____

18. If the existing purchase money trust deed is not assumable, will the lender agree to let us buy subject to the obligation? _____

    a. Principal amount of indebtedness $ _____

    b. 1. Payments made to: _____

       2. How often? _____

    c. Amount of each installment $ _____

    d. Interest at rate of: _____

    e. How is interest paid? _____

    f. Any balloon payments required in future? _____

    g. Can this instrument be assumed by a subsequent buyer? _____

    h. Can balance be prepaid without penalty at any time? _____

    i. Can this trust deed be subordinated to construction loans? _____

    j. Can portions of land be released without full payment? _____

    k. Is there a no-waste clause in the trust deed or other pertinent document? _____

    l. Can we substitute security if payments are restricted? _____

    m. Does trust deed preclude personal liability or deficiency judgment? _____

    n. Is trustee under trust deed acceptable to us? _____

    o. Is there an acceleration clause in the existing note or trust deed? _____

    p. Are there any other provisions we want stricken or modified? _____
    _____

19. Will owner carry a second trust deed or mortgage? _____

20. Other methods or instruments of financing: _____
    _____

21. Escrow and title company _____
    a. Escrow company: _____
    b. Title company: _____
    c. Assessment of their respective financial condition (obtain annual or quarterly reports): _____
    d. Are they acceptable to us and to the lenders? _____
    e. Does agreement provide that seller accepts responsibility for misappropriations or should we make our down payment check payable directly to seller? _____

22. Escrow officer: _____
    Address: _____
    Phone: _____

23. a. Duration of escrow: _____
    b. On what basis can we provide for extension of escrow? _____

24. a. Escrow fee split: buyer: _____% seller: _____%
    b. Transfer tax: buyer: _____ % seller: _____%
       Escrow deposit required by seller: _____
    c. How much of escrow deposit is forfeitable? _____
    d. When? _____
    e. On what basis? _____
    f. Are assessments to be paid in full by seller? _____
    g. Does seller pay all deferred taxes and interest? _____
    h. Who pays any deferred property taxes or interest on these taxes payable when land is developed?
       _____

25. What contingency clauses should be in Agreement/escrow instructions?

    ___ Approval of title in _____ days   ___ Access or easements
    ___ Approval by FHA, VA, or both   ___ Financing
    ___ Approval of soil report in _____ days   ___ Environmental impact approval
    ___ Approval of geology report in _____ days ___ Closing of another escrow
    ___ Approval of toxics study in _____ days   ___ Annexation
    ___ Approval of engineering study in _____ days ___ Building permits
    ___ Obtaining zone change by _____   ___ Condemnation
    ___ Obtaining general plan amendment by _____ ___ Moratoriums
    ___ Allocations of sewer   ___ Automatic extension if _____
    ___ Obtaining density of at least _____
    ___ Architectural Committee approval   ___ Approval of tentative
    ___ Approval of wetlands survey   map by _____
    ___ Availability of utilities   ___ Approval of final map by
    Other _____   _____

26. a. Who pays for proof of title? _____

    b. Type of title insurance policy or other assurance of title: _____

    c. Who pays for additional endorsements? _____

27. What warranties or other obligations does the seller have? _____
_____

28. Can we assign our escrow position to another buyer? _____

29. Will seller bear expense of settling boundaries? _____

30. Who pays for clearing easements or liens? _____

31. a. Are there groves or other crops on land? _____ What kind? _____

    b. Is there any smog control over burning trees? _____

    c. Is land used, or can it be used, for grazing? _____

        Remarks: _____

    d. Annual income: last year _____ year before _____ 2 years before _____

        Annual expenses: last year _____ year before _____ 2 years before _____

    e. Do we get smudge pots, wind machines, and crops? _____

    f. How long do we want to continue farming? _____

    g. 1. Does seller or existing trust deed require that we farm or permit continued farming, until payoff or harvest? _____

        2. If so, who is available to rent/farm land? _____

32. Describe briefly any other terms of the purchase agreement which are different from our standard agreement or present significant risks: _____
_____
_____

Additional Notes for Section 4:

5

Condition of Title

Compiled by: _____ Date: _____

1. Name of title company: _____ Officer: _____

   Address: _____ Phone: _____

2. a. Date preliminary title report (PTR) reviewed: _____

   b. Does PTR contain plot of property? _____

   c. What potential problems do the underlying documents reveal? _____

   d. List any discrepancies between the PTR and the state of title as represented by owner or broker: _____

   e. Source of legal description: _____

3. a. Describe any lis pendens (notice of pending litigation affecting title to the property) which have been filed: _____

   b. Should we do a litigation search on the owner? _____

   c. Has the owner recorded a disclaimer relating to toxics or hazardous wastes on the site (usually unacceptable to lenders)? _____

   d. Is there anything detrimental in title report which cannot be cleared before close of escrow? _____

   e. If yes, will owner post a bond with or indemnify title company? _____

4. a. Could there be other ownership (a "spite strip" for example) between subject land and road, utility, access, etc. ? _____

   b. Do we have title report on adjoining land? _____

5. Are there any agricultural preserve contracts in force? _____

   a. What is the scope and duration of the agreement? _____

   b. What is the likelihood and cost of buying out the parties? _____

   c. Will the owner agree to pay the cost of buying out the parties?

6. Describe any other agreements affecting the site (maintenance contract, use agreement, leases, etc.): _____

Agreement	When Recorded	Impact on Development
_____	_____	_____
_____	_____	_____
_____	_____	_____

7. a. Restrictions recorded in:

Type	County	Book	Page	Date
____	_____	____	____	____
____	_____	____	____	____

    b. Describe restrictions which pose problems (such as a "no liquor" covenant or an objectional design requirement): _____

    c. What remedy exists with respect to those restrictions? _____

8. Assessments (improvements):

Type	Amount Payable	How Often?	Total balance due
____	_____	_____	_____
____	_____	_____	_____
____	_____	_____	_____
____	_____	_____	_____

9. a. List all easements, (including public utility easements):

      1. _____
      2. _____
      3. _____
      4. _____

    b. Characteristics of these easements:

	1.	2.	3.	4.
Have we read the easement description?	___	___	___	___
Has it been plotted on a map?	___	___	___	___
Width of easement:	___	___	___	___
Can we build in it?	___	___	___	___
Can roads cross it?	___	___	___	___
Will it cause problems in development?	___	___	___	___
When does this easement terminate?	___	___	___	___

    c. Additional comments: _____

    d. Should the area of easements be subtracted in computing net acreage? _____

    e. Describe any existing obligation to grant additional easements: _____

    f. Are we absolutely certain detrimental easements can be cleared prior to close of escrow? _____

10. Property taxes:
    a. Taxes per year $ _____ Tax rate $ _____ per $100
    b. Tax assessor's valuation $ _____ based upon _____% of market value

11. a. List mineral, gas, oil, water, and other rights which go with the land: _____

    b. 1. Any reserved mineral or oil and gas rights of record (special concern of FHA, VA, and lender)? _____
        2. Will holder of rights quit-claim at least surface entry and first 500 feet (FHA, VA, and many lenders require this)? _____
        3. If not, can title insurance endorsement be provided against surface entry? _____

    c. 1. Who is lessor? _____
        2. Who is lessee? _____
        3. Terms of lease: _____

12. Are there any existing trust deed liens (other than those listed in Purchase Agreement Data)? _____

13. Other liens (other than existing trust deed liens): _____
    a. Mechanic's liens: _____
    b. Tax liens: _____
    c. Judgment liens: _____
    d. Other: _____

14. Which liens are to be cleared by owner prior to closing the transaction? _____

Additional Notes for Section 5:

6

Physical Aspects

Compiled by: _____ Date: _____

Note: Some items in this section can be completed by referring to documents; however, the land should be walked—not merely driven past. It is not necessary to cover every square inch, but do not solely walk the perimeter. Evidence of vehicle tracks should be followed to look for signs of illicit dumping on or just off the land. Also, be critical of your sources of information, and think about the possibility that your source of information could be inaccurate or incomplete (for example, mere observation of the site at any particular time may not reveal the existence of a *seasonal watercourse* which could create a flood, drainage, or wetlands problem; a document which you review may be outdated.)

1. Size of property: _____

2. Altitude of land: _____ feet

3. a. Is there a topo map available? _____

   b. If aerial topo, do we question its accuracy? _____

   c. If not aerial topo, what type of topo is it? _____

   d. Describe any problems apparent from the topo map: _____
      _____

   e. Is fall in the right direction in order to drain away from adjacent developed property? _____

   f. Can site be properly drained without excessive mitigation? _____

   g. Without building retaining walls? _____

   h. Percentage of land level: _____ rolling: _____ sloping: _____ steep: _____

   i. Percentage of land which might be lost due to easements _____ vertical slopes _____
      swamp or other water _____
      deep gorges or washes _____ roads _____ other _____

   j. Total area which should be excluded in computing net acreage to be paid for: _____

4. a. Has land been surveyed? _____

   b. Surveyor and date of survey: _____

   c. Is plat available? _____

   d. Are exact boundary lines and corners known? _____

   e. Will neighbors cooperate in settling boundaries? _____

   f. If a record of survey of adjoining or nearby properties exists, what is the affect on this property?
      _____

5. Describe any portion of land that is in any special regulatory zones, such as coastal commission:

   coastal commision: _____   national forest: _____

   fire hazard area: _____   wildlife preserve: _____

   U.S. Army Corps of Engineers: _____   air quality management district: _____

   nuclear power plant Basic

   Emergency Planning Zone: _____   other: _____

6. Describe any portion of the land that has been, or may be classified as a historic landmark, or as a paleontologically, historically, culturally, or archaeologically significant site by federal, state, or local government: _____
   _____

7. a. Consultant and date of soil report: _____
   b. Was testing extensive enough, or do we need to do additional tests? _____
   _____

   c. What percentage of site has been filled? _____
   d. Problem soil—expansive clay: _____ rocky: _____ adobe: _____ arsenic: _____ caliche–hard: _____ caliche–soft: _____ sulfate: _____ gravel: _____ cemented gravel: _____ alkali: _____ salt: _____ conglomerate: _____ other: _____
   e. What additional tests are needed? _____
   _____

   f. Are there any soil conditions which may cause excessive building costs or problems, such as the need for a reinforced slab (attach summary from soils report)? _____
   _____

   g. How much import soil will be necessary? _____
   h. How much export will be necessary? _____
   i. If we choose not to test the site, do we have available soil reports from adjacent or nearby properties? _____

8. Local engineer's advice: _____
   _____
   _____

9. Local soils engineer/geologist's advice: _____
   _____
   _____

10. a. Consultant and date of geology report: _____
    b. State earthquake map for the area? _____

c. Are active earthquake faults shown and what is the criteria for an active fault? _____

d. Are inferred faults shown? _____

e. Should active faults shown be extended (inferred) onto this land? _____

f. Describe any special building setbacks that will apply as a result of proximity to one or more faults: _____

g. Geologist's estimate of cost to overcome any indicated problem? _____

h. Describe any federal, state, or local laws or regulations pertaining to faults which will impact on the development: _____

11. a. Are there any natural or man-made bodies of water? _____

b. Does water run year-round? _____

c. Are there flood hazards? _____

d. In what Federal Emergency Management Agency's Flood Insurance Rate Map Zone is this land? _____

e. Is zone a problem to us, a potential buyer, or lender? _____

f. Describe how we can get the land reclassified or mitigate the problem in some other way: _____

12. a. Current and past uses and nature of surrounding land:

North _____

East _____

South _____

West _____

b. Explain any environmental problems arising out of the nature and/or uses of this surrounding land: _____

13. a. Consultant and date of wetlands report: _____

b. How much of the land is shown as wetlands on U. S. Fish and Wildlife Service's National Wetland Inventory Maps? _____

c. Do Corps of Engineers and Environmental Protection Agency agree on the delineation? _____

d. Are there any blue lines and/or marsh symbols on the USGS topo map for this site? _____

e. Are there any indications that water may stand on property part of the year so that the land could later be designated as wetlands (look for gray or blackish soil, and orange spots from dried-out iron)? _____

f. Have you observed any swales (low contour areas that pass water) or channels (beds with defined banks) on the site? _____

g. If portions of the site are delineated as wetlands, can we qualify for a designation by the Corps of Engineers that our activity is covered under a nationwide permit? _____

h. If yes, have we had the Corps of Engineers verify (1) that less than an acre of wetlands exists on our property and (2) that there is authority for us to proceed under a nationwide permit? _____

i. Has the appropriate state agency for wetlands asserted jurisdiction over the land? _____

j. If yes, what are its requirements? _____

14. a. Consultant and date of biologist's report (attach summary of report): _____

b. Name(s) of any possibly endangered species on site: _____

c. Classification of species: endangered _____ threatened _____ candidate _____

d. Source of information: _____

e. Agencies contacted: _____

f. Describe the habitat set-aside requirement or other possible mitigation measures: _____

15. a. What percentage of the site or any adjacent site is affected by scaled broomweed (a type of noxious plant whose invasive root system can crack concrete and which is difficult to completely eradicate)? _____

b. Name and date of consultant report which verifies presence of scaled broomweed: _____

c. Are there any trees (such as Oak, or Joshua) on the land which are either protected by law or may otherwise be difficult to move? _____

d. Is a permit required to move trees? _____

e. From whom is it obtained? _____

f. How long will it take to obtain it? _____

16. a. Consultant and date of hazardous materials report: _____

b. Describe any physical signs of possible waste dumping on the land, such as, discolored soil or soft, dying vegetation, debris, etc.: _____

c. Describe any above or below ground gasoline, fuel oil, or other chemical storage tanks, drums, or pipelines on the site: _____

d. Which ones have been tested for leakage? _____

e. Has contaminated soil, if any, been remediated? _____

f. If asbestos is present, is it "friable" (brittle and loose in the air where it can be inhaled)? _____

g. Does it have to be removed or can it be left in place safely? _____

h. Are there any structures which may contain asbestos or other hazardous materials? _____

i. Are there any old transformers, capacitors, or other equipment on the site which may indicate the presence of PCB's (polychlorinated biphenyls, a group of synthetic organic compounds used for insulation of electrical components, which become dangerous to living things when released into the air or water)? _____

j. How far away are nearby high voltage lines (electric or magnetic field health risk) and what is their current capacity/voltage? _____

k. Should we consider a disclosure regarding electrical or magnetic fields in our sales contracts for homes we build on this land? _____

l. What is the condition of the groundwater under the site? _____

m. Are there drill holes on the land? _____

n. Are the wells capped per state requirements? _____

o. What conditions indicate further testing is needed? _____

p. What is needed in terms of time and cost to clean up the site, and what chance exists of finding more problems as clean-up progresses? _____

q. What agencies are to be involved in the clean-up? _____

17. a. Check the sources you have used, independent of consultant, to become aware of possible hazardous materials or wastes on the site from past uses:

walk around: _____

aerial photos: _____

informal inquiry of government agencies: _____

other: _____

b. Do any government toxic site lists identify this property or other property within 2,000 feet? _____

c. Has the site ever been the subject of an investigation or citation for violation of any environmental laws? _____

d. Any other known or apparent risk from current or previous handling, disposal, or storage of hazardous or toxic material on site or on adjacent land? _____

e. Do we have any test results or reports available (attach summary of environmental audit)? _____

f. Were clean-up measures undertaken in the past and by whom? _____

g. Which public agencies have issued or could issue certificates of non-contamination? _____

h. Distance to and nature of nearest industrial facilities: _____

i. How far away is the nearest chemical plant or dump? _____

j. How far away are any landfills? _____

k. Any evidence of methane in area? _____

18. a. Is the property over any mines? _____
    If yes, is the depth-to-mine less than 300 feet? _____

b. Does the land surface have one or more shallow depressions, recent open cracks, or enlarging sink holes? _____

c. Is land in or near radon belt as shown on EPA map or in the opinion of soils engineer (attach soils report)? _____

d. If not on map, what are conclusions of environmental testing? _____

e. What can be done to mitigate and what will it cost? _____

f. Should we consider a disclosure regarding radon in our sales contracts for homes built on this land? _____

19. a. Summarize the special problems or issues you foresee with respect to the impact of our project on the environment: _____

b. What measures can we take to mitigate the impact? _____

c. What are the costs associated with such mitigation? _____

_____

20. a. Describe any contemplated design aspects that will require a grant of easement or other cooperation or permission from any off-site landowner in connection with development of the site? _____

_____

_____

Aspect of Development	Owner	Nature of Consent (must be in writing and recorded *before* money is released)
grading:	_____	_____
drainage:	_____	_____
access during construction:	_____	_____
right-of-way easements:	_____	_____
	_____	_____
other: _____	_____	_____
_____	_____	_____

b. Do we have any reason to doubt the authority of the owner to grant such permission? _____

c. In connection with required easements or rights-of-way, have we obtained subordination to our easement from the holders of any prior liens or encumbrances? _____
Explain any problems: _____

_____

d. If there are public rights-of-way, which agency owns each? _____

_____

e. If more than one agency owns rights-of-way, or the owner is other than the agency doing the plan checking, how does this multiple ownership affect our timing and procedure for plan check and final approval? _____

f. Is there any evidence of possible prescriptive easements, such as pipelines or footpaths in areas not plotted as easements? _____

_____

21. Road rights-of-way:
   a. 1. Private/public: _____

2. If road is private (or if there are no roads), is there a legally acceptable right of ingress and egress? _____

    b. Improved? _____

    c. Master-planned widths? _____

    d. Can roads be vacated or moved? _____

    e. Should the areas of road rights-of-way be subtracted in computing net acreage to be paid for? _____

22. a. Does land have any road frontage? _____ feet: _____

    b. Surface of road: _____

    c. Road classification: _____

    d. How near to our site is any proposed freeway or highway? _____

    e. When is construction of the freeway or highway scheduled to begin? _____ To be completed? _____

    f. Does land have access to a dedicated road? _____

    g. Is access sufficient? _____

    h. Is land accessible during all seasons of year? _____

    Remarks: _____

23. a. Vegetation growth is: light _____ moderate _____ heavy _____

    b. Is overall vegetation a help or hindrance? _____

    c. Quantity of any marketable timber or trees: _____

24. a. Are there existing perimeter walls on the site that will be affected by the development process? _____

    b. Are we likely to be able to add to the walls or be able to match our grade to the existing grade? _____

25. Is the property within 2,000 feet from the end of a runway or in the flight path of a commercial airport or military airfield? _____

26. Is the property within a line-of-sight distance of 1,000 feet* from a highway (four or more lanes)? _____

27. If there are conditions around the site that could create excessive noise, have we determined that the noise level is not in excess of 65 L_{dn}* (formula for averaging day/night noise; check with acoustical engineer)? _____

---

*These are 1985 standards for the U.S. Department of Housing and Urban Development (HUD) Appraiser/Review Appraiser Checksheet. OMB2502-0327.

28. Specify if the controlling agency has more stringent standards from HUD for proximity to:

   airports: _____; distance from highway: _____;

   noise levels: _____; distance from railroad tracks: _____.

29. Are there railroad tracks on or within 3,000* feet of the site? _____

   a. Name of railroad which owns the tracks: _____

   b. Main line or spur: _____

   c. How close is the nearest railroad terminal? _____

   d. Number of trips per day past our site: _____

   e. Speed at which trains travel past our site: _____

   f. Is there coupling/uncoupling near our site? _____

   g. Is there a crossing near our site? _____

   h. Does the proximity of the railroad create problems of noise or vibration for our development?
   _____

   i. Whether the railroad tracks are on-site, contiguous, or nearby, describe any pipelines within the railroad right-of-way (such as, gas, electric, liquids, etc.): _____

   j. Will any improvements need to be constructed in the railroad right-of-way?

      1. Grading: _____

      2. Streets: _____

      3. Water: _____

      4. Walls: _____

      5. Electric: _____

      6. Sewer: _____

      7. Storm drainage: _____

      8. Other: _____

   k. Have we secured the necessary easements? _____

   l. Will new crossing arms be required? _____

   m. If we have to relocate the tracks, describe the process, time frame, cost, and availability of governmental assistance: _____

   n. What can be done to expedite any required approvals or agreement with the railroad? _____

30. Explain any special issues or problems in connection with the neighbors, utilities, open space, other:
   _____

31. a. Special hazards and nuisances—use the following checklist to highlight and summarize the special hazards, nuisances, or environmental issues which impact the land. Tell how problems can be mitigated:

Condition	NO	YES	If "yes," explain how we could mitigate:
Power lines	___	___	_____
Communication towers	___	___	_____
"HAM" operators	___	___	_____
Soil erosion or subsidence	___	___	_____
Earthquake fault	___	___	_____
Poor soils	___	___	_____
Rock/grading issues	___	___	_____
High vehicular traffic	___	___	_____
Air traffic/flight pattern	___	___	_____
Airport	___	___	_____
Military base	___	___	_____
Explosives	___	___	_____
Noise or vibration	___	___	_____
Fire hazard (brush, etc.)	___	___	_____
Fire stations	___	___	_____
Smoke, fumes or odors	___	___	_____
Poor surface drainage	___	___	_____
Flood hazard	___	___	_____
Flood control channels	___	___	_____
High water table	___	___	_____
Nearby factories and/or refineries	___	___	_____
Unsightly views	___	___	_____
Dam upstream	___	___	_____
TV interference	___	___	_____
Nearby open canal	___	___	_____
Dumping of junk and debris	___	___	_____
Toxics on site	___	___	_____
Nearby chemical hazards	___	___	_____

Condition	NO	YES	If "yes," explain how we could mitigate:
Nearby rock/gravel quarry	——	——	————————————————
Wetlands on site	——	——	————————————————
Heavy winds	——	——	————————————————
Railroad tracks	——	——	————————————————
Protected trees on site	——	——	————————————————
Endangered species on site	——	——	————————————————
Nearby incompatibly zoned land	——	——	————————————————
Barriers to direct sun	——	——	————————————————
More than 30-minute commute to nearest metropolitan center	——	——	————————————————
Any other concerns that might deter buyers	——	——	————————————————

b. To which of these hazards will FHA, VA, other lenders, or governmental agencies object? _____

Additional Notes for Section 6:

7

Utility Availability

Compiled by: _____ Date: _____

1. If our site is in a master planned community, do we agree with the location of the utilities? _____

2. If placement of utilities has been completed, are there easements for the utilities? _____
   Are they of record? _____

3.
   a. Nearest gas line at distance of: _____
   b. Capacity to serve property? _____
   c. Name of utility company (see attached cost estimate): _____
   d. Front-end advance required: $ _____
   e. When, and on what basis, is amount refundable? _____
   f. Have we obtained a copy of the refunding or oversize allowance agreements? _____
   g. Name and phone number of contact person at utility: _____
   h. Has a moratorium been imposed or considered? _____

4.
   a. Nearest electrical line at distance of: _____
   b. Capacity to serve property? _____
   c. Name of utility company (see attached cost estimate): _____
   d. Front-end advance required: $ _____
   e. When, and on what basis, is amount refundable? _____
   f. Name and phone number of contact person at utility: _____
   g. Have we obtained a copy of the refunding or oversize allowance agreements? _____
   h. Has a moratorium been imposed or considered? _____

5.
   a. Nearest water line at distance of: _____
   b. Is water furnished by public or private utility? _____
      Name of water company (see attached cost estimate): _____
   c. Name and phone number of contact person at utility: _____
   d. What amount of contribution, if any, will we be required to make toward the upkeep of the existing facilities? _____

e. What are the conditions of service? _____

f. Does the water system require us to use its contractor to install the system on our site? _____
If so, what is the cost to us? _____

g. Are there governmental restrictions (including fire department) on construction of model homes before the water system is fully functional? _____

h. Is there capacity and sufficient pressure in the system to serve our development, including two-story houses? _____

i. Can the existing system's water be used for development and construction? _____

j. What special requirements or restrictions exist in connection with use of water on our site (water rationing, for example?) _____

k. Is installation of a water line a condition of obtaining building permits? _____
For models as well? _____

l. Do we need to loop the water system? _____

m. Is the water quality satisfactory? _____

n. Are water tests available? _____

o. Specific water source (well, river, etc.): _____

p. Front-end advance required: $ _____

q. When, and on what basis, is amount refundable? _____

r. Have we obtained a copy of the refunding or oversize allowance agreements? _____

s. Has a moratorium been imposed or considered? _____

6. a. What governmental bodies or other agencies have jurisdiction over water on or around our site? _____

b. If special permits are required for connecting to the water line:
   1. Time period to acquire: _____
   2. Cost to acquire: $ _____
   3. What special studies are required? _____
   4. Which agency will review our application? _____

5. If any other agencies are involved in the review process, does the timing, cost, or criteria for review differ from the lead agency? Explain for each agency: _____

_____

_____

c. Who will own and maintain any on-site water lines? _____

d. Which entities will require easements from us? _____

7. a. Does land have or need water rights? _____

b. Do we have or need water stock? _____

c. Cost of needed water stock available for purchase: $ _____

8. a. Any wells on land? _____ pumping at depth of _____ feet

b. Nearest wells to land at distance of _____ pumping at depth of _____ feet

c. Estimated depth of ground water in immediate area: _____

d. Are there any reservoirs on or adjacent to the land? _____

e. Are there any streams on or adjacent to the land? _____

f. Conclusions of available test results regarding pollutants or toxic chemicals in ground water from wells or streams on the land or in the immediate area: _____

_____

g. If there are no water lines nearby, can we dig individual wells? _____

h. Can we dig a community well? _____

i. What restrictions will be imposed by the state and county health departments? _____

9. Type of sewage disposal facilities required/allowable in area: _____

_____

10. a. Nearest sewer line at distance of: _____

b. Public or private sewers? _____

c. Is a new line or treatment plant expansion required for capacity to serve property? _____

d. Estimated size of pumping plant or lift station needed to reach sewer: _____

e. Does the location of the lift station impact our site? _____

f. Can we redesign our tract to eliminate the need for a lift station? _____

g. Can a community septic tank or package plant be used here? _____

h. What is the cost of joining the sewer district (see attached cost estimate)? _____

i. Name and phone number of contact person at utility: _____

_____

j. Front-end advance required: $ _____

k. When, and on what basis, is amount refundable? _____
_____

l. Have we obtained a copy of the refunding or oversize allowance agreements? _____

m. Has a moratorium been imposed or considered? _____

n. What governmental bodies or other agencies have jurisdiction over sewer lines on or around our site? _____

o. If there are existing lines, who owns the sewer lines and facilities? _____

p. Who maintains the sewer lines? _____

q. If special permits are required for connecting to the sewer line:
   1. Time period to acquire: _____
   2. Cost to acquire: $ _____
   3. What special studies are required? _____
   4. Which agency will review our application? _____
   5. If any agencies are involved in the review process, does the timing, cost, or criteria for review differ from the lead agency? Explain for each agency: _____
   _____
   _____

r. Which entities will require easements from us? _____

s. Is installation of a sewer line a condition of obtaining building permits? _____ For models as well? _____

11. a. Telephone company: _____
    b. Special notes: _____
    _____

12. a. Cable TV company: _____
    b. Special notes: _____
    _____

13. a. What are the standards for private/public street lights? _____
    What special types of lights are required? _____
    b. What types of plans are required from us in connection with public street lights? _____
    Private street lights? _____
    _____
    c. Who maintains street lights? _____
    d. Do we pay for the street light electricity, if so, for how long? _____

14. a. Storm drain or flood control required? _____

    b. Are existing lines at sufficient depths and capacity to handle our development? _____

    c. Can we use a temporary retention/detention basin until master facilities are available? _____

    d. If there are existing lines, who owns the storm drain facility? _____

    e. Who maintains the storm drain facilities? _____

    f. Do they agree with our design? _____

    g. What governmental bodies or other agencies have jurisdiction over storm drainage on or around our site? _____

    h. If special permits are required for connecting to the existing facilities:

        1. Time period to acquire: _____

        2. Cost to acquire: $ _____

        3. What special studies are required? _____

        4. What are the specified times of the year for tie-ins? _____

        5. Which agency will review our application to tie-in? _____

        6. If any agencies are involved in the review process, does the timing, cost, or criteria for review differ from the lead agency? Explain for each agency: _____

    i. Which entities will require easements from us? _____

    j. Is installation of a storm drain a condition of obtaining building permits? _____ For models as well? _____

15. a. Police, fire, trash pick-up services provided by local entity? _____

    b. What is fire insurance rating? _____

    c. If no public fire department exists, is there a volunteer or privately contracted fire protection agency? _____

    d. What are the requirements of the fire department with respect to water, street width, and access? _____

    e. Is residential sprinkler requirement in force or being considered? _____

16. All utilities:

    a. Which utilities allow joint trenching? _____

    b. Do we have to relocate or underground any of the above utility lines, if so, which lines? _____

c. Which utilities will pay for any or all of the cost? _____

d. Which adjoining landowners should share utility costs with us and will agree to do so? _____

e. For which utilities could we install our own utility systems? _____

f. If land is in a county, for which utilities could we connect to the city system without annexing? _____

g. For which utilities are there any additional or unusual costs if we are outside the city or urban area? _____

17. a. Have we contacted all of the departments or agencies which will need to comment, approve, or be involved in the design of each utility? _____
    b. The installation of each utility? _____
    c. The maintenance of each utility? _____

Additional Notes for Section 7:

8

Entitlements

Compiled by: _____ Date: _____

1. What is the governing body? _____
2. a. Is the site part of an already established master planned community? _____
   b. If yes, describe the implications in connection with entitlements: _____
3. a. Is the developer required to provide any municipal facilities or maintenance services? _____
   b. Will the governing body permit private streets? _____
   c. Will the governing body permit gates? _____
4. a. What is the attitude of the governing body and local citizens toward new development? _____
   b. If site is an in-fill project, have we talked informally with surrounding homeowners? _____ What has been their response? _____
   c. If not an in-fill site, what problems could we forestall by meeting with the surrounding homeowners to discuss our proposed project: _____
   d. Might our development engender opposition by blocking neighbors' views or because of incompatibility with neighboring uses? _____
   e. Are neighbors or the governing body likely to resist rezoning or general plan amendments? If so, why? _____
   f. Describe any pending or in-place moratoriums or development limitations: _____
   g. Can this land be processed to the point where permits can be obtained or our right to build becomes vested before the effective date of such moratoriums or limitations? _____
5. a. Is there a growth management plan? _____
   b. 1. Is there a community architectural review board? _____
      2. If so, how can we be named to the architectural committee? _____

c. Describe any in-process or proposed plans by any agency to widen the streets or build freeways or highways in a radius of five miles of our site: _____

d. Describe any anticipated or actual governmental requirements that will require us to obtain the cooperation or permission of any off-site landowner in connection with the development of our site (such as grading, drainage, easements, rights-of-way, street improvements, etc.): _____

6. a. Describe current and proposed city or county ordinances or any other regulations, amendments, restrictions, or requirements which impact adversely on our development (attach cost estimate):
   1. Subdivision: _____
   2. Building: _____
   3. Park dedication: _____
   4. Underground: _____
   5. Zoning: _____
   6. Solar: _____
   7. Growth management: _____
   8. Architectural restrictions: _____
   9. Lot size restrictions: _____
   10. Commercial or industrial limitations: _____
   11. Other: _____

   b. Describe any unusual or costly FHA requirements: _____

   c. Describe any unusual or costly VA requirements: _____

7. a. Does the local jurisdiction use the Uniform Building Code (if so, what year) or other type of standard code? _____

   b. Comments from discussion with local building department (Person contacted _____):
   _____
   _____
   _____

8. a. Are there any low-income housing requirements for the site? _____
   b. Will they accept payment in lieu of units? _____

9. a. Does the governing body require subdivision bonds? _____
   b. Will they accept a lender's agreement in lieu of bond? _____

c. Must lender be local, or special type? _____

d. Will they accept cash, a letter of credit, or other collateral? _____

e. Will governing body allow reasonable partial releases of subdivision collateral as work progresses? _____

10. a. Present zoning per ordinances: _____

b. General plan land use designation for site: _____

c. General plan use designation for surrounding area: _____

d. Is there a specific plan for the area? _____

e. Describe any aspects of any local plan that adversely affect our site: _____

f. Describe any conflict between the general plan, the zoning regulations, and the actual use of our site and the surrounding area: _____

g. If general plan amendment is necessary, how long will it take until the governing body processes such amendment? _____

h. Potential zoning change? _____

i. Zoning of surrounding land: _____

j. General plan/zoning ordinance being revised? _____

k. Any zone changes proposed nearby which would be detrimental to our proposed use of this land? _____

l. When and how has anyone nearby amended the general plan? _____

11. a. What does the planning department think of our site and our proposed development? (Person contacted: _____)

b. If seller is a developer and has already secured approval for development plans, what is the process and time frame if we wish to amend those plans? _____

c. Are we in a jurisdiction that will consider negotiating a development agreement? _____

d. Do we want a development agreement and, if so, how quickly could we negotiate one? _____

e. What is the process? _____

12. a. In which city's sphere of influence is the land? _____
    b. If land is in a county, can it be annexed to the city? _____
    c. Is it advantageous to annex? _____
13. a. Is there a tentative or final subdivision map on the land? _____
    b. 1. If tentative, when does it expire? _____
       2. Is extension possible? _____
    c. 1. Number of lots: _____
       2. Lot size: _____
    d. 1. Could we do a better layout? _____
       2. How much delay to change it? _____
    e. Describe any onerous conditions for subdivision map previously agreed to by seller or prior owner: _____
14. a. What other tentative maps have been filed in the area? _____
    b. By whom? _____
    c. For how many units? _____
    d. What have we learned about processing requirements from other developers? _____
15. a. Is land in a designated redevelopment area? _____
    b. Can we get special zoning, financing, or expediting? _____
16. a. Is land being considered for public use? _____
    b. Is land now under condemnation? _____
    c. If land is now under condemnation, to what extent will we have to get involved in the condemnation process? _____
17. Is land use controlled by a homeowners association? _____
18. Is there a required donation of land, cash, or cash in lieu of land for open space, parks, schools, sewers, or recreation (attach cost estimate)? _____
19. On what basis can we receive credit toward open space requirements? _____
20. a. Names of school districts: (1) _____
                                  (2) _____
    b. What is the attitude of the school districts toward development? _____

c. Is there a school impaction problem which may result in imposition of fees or a moratorium on building permits? _____

d. Amount of established impaction fee: _____

e. Are the existing facilities adequate to serve our project? _____

f. Are existing facilities permanent or temporary? _____

g. If temporary, source of funding for permanent facilities: _____

21. a. Describe nature of, proposed amount, and proposed time for any fee increases not yet in effect: _____

b. Can we prepay fees before the increase? _____

c. What approvals are needed before payment? _____

d. Are there any exceptions we could fall under, or is there any basis for negotiating a lower rate, performing construction work, or providing temporary facilities in lieu of cash payment of capital facilities fee? _____

e. Describe any existing agreements whereby the seller prepaid specific fees, and whether, when, and in what amounts we will need to reimburse seller: _____

22. Describe any governmental requirements which must be met before closing the sale of the first unit which could be a problem (include off-site requirements): _____

23. List reports required by applicable agency and the preparer of such report:

Report	Agency	Prepared By:
Environmental impact report: _____	_____	_____
Traffic: _____	_____	_____
Noise: _____	_____	_____
Biological: _____	_____	_____
Specialized soil studies: _____	_____	_____
Toxics: _____	_____	_____
Tree removal: _____	_____	_____
Utilities: _____	_____	_____
Grading: _____	_____	_____
Other: _____	_____	_____

24. a. Will we need to do a full Environmental Impact Report? _____

    If not, describe what will be required: _____

    b. What are the time frames for the environmental impact report process:

    1. Initial study: _____
    2. Preparation: _____
    3. Public notice: _____
    4. Public hearings: _____
    5. Certification: _____

    c. Explain how any of the requirements of the local air quality management control district present problems for our proposed development: _____

25. If our site is within the jurisdiction of an airport land use commission, coastal commission, air quality control commission, or similar commission, name the agency and describe any requirements that impact on our proposed development: _____

26. Whom could we contact for political help if needed? _____

27. Is there an expedited process for models? _____ How many units may be started before final approval of the tentative map? _____

28. a. Does the governmental entity do the plan check itself or contract out (if contracted, to whom)? _____

    b. Is plan check deposit partially refundable or applicable to work in other departments? _____
    c. Will agency provide statement of hours and charges for checking? _____
    d. Can we pay overtime to speed plan checking? _____

29. a. Is the property within a community facilities assessment district? _____
    b. What are the current assessments? _____
    c. Are there any proposed assessments? _____
    d. Can we form or join assessment districts to finance development? _____
    e. How can we get out of existing assessment districts? _____

30. a. Identify each step in the subdivision approval process, the approximate time it takes for each step, and what body or agency must approve (note key dates on Summary Routing Schedule):

Approval Required: Annexation

Agency, District,
or Development: _____

Time Frame: _____

Contact: _____ Phone: _____

Approval Required: General plan amendment

Agency, District,
or Development: _____

Time Frame: _____

Contact: _____ Phone: _____

Approval Required: Environmental Impact Report

Agency, District,
or Development: _____

Time Frame: _____

Contact: _____ Phone: _____

Approval Required: Rezoning

Agency, District,
or Development: _____

Time Frame: _____

Contact: _____ Phone: _____

Approval Required: Variance

Agency, District,
or Development: _____

Time Frame: _____

Contact: _____ Phone: _____

Approval Required: Conditional use permit

Agency, District,
    or Development: _____

Time Frame: _____

Contact: _____ Phone: _____

Approval Required: Tentative map

Agency, District,
    or Development: _____

Time Frame: _____

Contact: _____ Phone: _____

Approval Required: Recordation of final map

Agency, District,
    or Development: _____

Time Frame: _____

Contact: _____ Phone: _____

Approval Required: Other (specify)

Agency, District,
    or Development: _____

Time Frame: _____

Contact: _____ Phone: _____

b.   Which of the above items can be processed concurrently? _____

c.   If our proposed project is a planned-use development, explain any special requirements for the tentative map or any other aspect of the approval process that may impact us adversely: _____

Additional Notes for Section 8:

9

Development Costs

(Estimated by: _____ Date: _____)

It is assumed that cost estimates will be prepared on a computer to allow for ease of revision as information is updated throughout the development process and the addition of greater detail as to the specific fee or cost. The following is an extensive (but not exhaustive) list of the types of items that might be included depending on the type of project and locale:

	Preliminary Date _____	**Revised** Date _____
1. Permits, fees, etc.:		
DRE public report fees	$_____	$_____
Permits and plan check	_____	_____
Inspection and review fees	_____	_____
Growth management fees	_____	_____
Capital facilities fees	_____	_____
Conditional use permit	_____	_____
Development taxes	_____	_____
Sewer connection fees	_____	_____
Sewer treatment fees	_____	_____
Sanitation district fees	_____	_____
Storm drainage fees	_____	_____
Water connection fees	_____	_____
Break-up (storage) facilities fees	_____	_____
Treatment fees	_____	_____
Annexation fees	_____	_____
School fees	_____	_____
Fire mitigation fees	_____	_____
Park fees	_____	_____
Beautification fees	_____	_____
Bond premiums	_____	_____
Tentative map fees	_____	_____
Final map fees	_____	_____
Variance fees	_____	_____
General plan amendment fees	_____	_____

Zone change fees _____ _____

Health permit _____ _____

School district fee _____ _____

Environmental Impact Report review fee _____ _____

Any other fees not listed above: _____ _____

_____ _____ _____

_____ _____ _____

_____ _____ _____

_____ _____ _____

2. Engineering:

    Civil engineering and surveying $_____ $_____

    Soils/geological engineering _____ _____

    Utilities consultant _____ _____

    Sound engineering _____ _____

    Environmental consultant _____ _____

    Traffic engineering _____ _____

    Landscape engineering _____ _____

    Wetlands assessment _____ _____

    Biological consultant _____ _____

    Horticulture consultant _____ _____

3. Clearing and grading:

    Demolition and clearing $_____ $_____

    Relocation of utilities, structures, etc. _____ _____

    Excavation and rough grading _____ _____

    Grading pads _____ _____

    Over-excavation _____ _____

    Soil import/export _____ _____

    Slope control and retaining walls _____ _____

    Rock/caliche removal _____ _____

    Hazardous material removal _____ _____

4. Sewage/drainage/water:

    Sewer lines $_____ $_____

    Septic tanks and cesspools   _____   _____

    Off-tract costs—sewer   _____   _____

    Storm drain lines   _____   _____

    Drainage structures (culverts, etc.)   _____   _____

    Off-tract costs—storm drains   _____   _____

    Pumping plants   _____   _____

    Water mains and hydrants   _____   _____

    Off-tract costs—water   _____   _____

    Water meters   _____   _____

5. Underground utilities (electricity, telephone, cable TV, gas):

    Trenching $_____ $_____

    Utility systems   _____   _____

6. Street work:

    Curbs and gutters $_____ $_____

    Sidewalks   _____   _____

    Driveways   _____   _____

    Median islands   _____   _____

    Other concrete work   _____   _____

    Paving   _____   _____

    Street lights   _____   _____

    Street signs   _____   _____

    Barricades   _____   _____

    Traffic signals   _____   _____

    Other street work   _____   _____

7. Other improvements:

    Perimeter landscaping $_____ $_____

    Park improvements   _____   _____

    Trails and bike paths   _____   _____

    Trees

    Perimeter block walls

    Other perimeter fences

    Bridges

    Lighting

    Holding ponds

    Miscellaneous

8. Total off-site costs

    Less: Refundable deposits $_____ $_____

          Costs benefitting other land or later units   (_____)   (_____)

    Plus: Carrying cost, indirects, and overhead

          Costs allocated from other land or earlier units

9. Total land and development cost $_____ $_____

    Estimated number of lots

10. Finished lot cost (each) $_____ $_____

    Estimated retail value of finished lot $_____ $_____

Additional Notes for Section 9:

10

Market Area and Proposed Product

Compiled by: _____ Date: _____

1. a. What do we propose to build on the property? _____
   b. Is the site large enough to build more than one product line? _____

   Plan _____, _____ s. f., $ _____   Plan _____, _____ s. f., $ _____

   Plan _____, _____ s. f., $ _____   Plan _____, _____ s. f., $ _____

   Plan _____, _____ s. f., $ _____   Plan _____, _____ s. f., $ _____

   c. How many sales per month should we expect? _____
   d. Should we be in two or more price ranges? _____
   e. Is there a niche or hole in the market we should fill? _____
   f. Is there an alternative use for this land if the proposed project doesn't pencil out? _____
   _____

2. a. Whom will we sell or rent to? _____
   b. Where will they work? _____
   c. How will they find us? _____

3. a. How many new or proposed units for sale or rent are within:

   15 Miles _____   5 Miles _____   1 Mile _____

   b. Absorption rate last year in market area: _____
   c. Estimated price range of homes: from $ _____ to $ _____
   d. Is the demand in the immediate area over-saturated by the supply of similarly subdivided properties offered for sale? _____

4. a. Is our site part of an already established planned community? _____
   b. Describe any master marketing program: _____
   c. What did the competing builders pay for land? _____
   d. Describe any other marketing implications of being part of a master planned community: _____
   _____

5. Why are existing developments selling or not selling? _____
   _____

6. Why can we compete or not compete with existing builders in the area? _____
   _____

7. What recreational facilities do we need to provide to be competitive? _____
_____
_____

8. a. What ethnic groups are part of our target market? _____
   b. Are there any characteristics in the design of our plan which might appeal to, or be offensive to, any ethnic or racial group's cultural beliefs? _____

9. a. Comparable sales:
   1. Date: _____ Location: _____ Acreage: _____
      Status of zoning, etc.: _____ Price: $ _____ acre
   2. Date: _____ Location: _____ Acreage: _____
      Status of zoning, etc.: _____ Price: $ _____ acre
   b. Analyze price per acre (or per lot or foot) with similar land offered for sale or recently sold in area: _____
   _____
   c. When would this land be ready for the development stage? Immediately: _____
      1-3 years: _____ 3-5 years: _____ 5-10 years: _____ Over 10 years: _____
   d. Distance and estimated time for development to reach this general area:
      _____
   e. What did this land or comparable land sell for 1 year ago? $ _____ 3 years ago? $ _____
      5 years ago? $ _____
   f. Are there indications that prices will increase in the future? _____
   g. Are any tax advantages associated with this land and/or our proposed project (rehabilitation tax credits, etc.)? _____
   _____

10. Residential lot subdivisions (unimproved) in area:
    a. Lot size: _____ Price $ _____ Location: _____
       What utilities/streets, etc. ? _____
    b. Lot size: _____ Price $ _____ Location: _____
       What utilities/streets, etc. ? _____

11. a. How many older residential developments are there within the market area, and what is the condition of each? _____
    _____
    b. What is the potential market for move-ups from the older homes? _____
    c. Resale price range of homes: from $ _____ to $ _____

d. Is the resale market strong or weak? _____

12. a. Any outstanding residential attributes of our land? _____

    b. How does the tax rate compare with competing areas? _____

13. Retirement community potential:
    a. How far are adequate hospital facilities? _____
    b. How many practicing medical doctors nearby? _____
    c. Proximity of golf courses, parks, libraries, and other community facilities: _____

14. Existing commercial and industrial developments nearby:

	Type	Approximate age	Distance from Land
a. Commercial	_____	_____	_____
	_____	_____	_____
	_____	_____	_____

	Type	Approximate age	Distance from Land
b. Industrial	_____	_____	_____
	_____	_____	_____
	_____	_____	_____

    c. Name, type, and scheduled date of completion of new industry under construction or planned: _____

    d. What is the likelihood of increased employment in the next few years? _____

15. Effect of military or other government installations nearby: _____

16. a. Existing and proposed shopping facilities nearby:

	Type	Approximate age	Distance from Land
Neighborhood (small)	_____	_____	_____
Local (medium)	_____	_____	_____
Regional (large)	_____	_____	_____

    b. New shopping facilities under construction or planned: _____

17. a. Schools:

	Name	Approximate age	Distance from Land	Transportation
Elementary	_____	_____	_____	_____
Junior High	_____	_____	_____	_____
High school	_____	_____	_____	_____
College/University	_____	_____	_____	_____

    b. New schools under construction or planned: _____
_____

    c. Parochial or other private schools: _____
_____

18. List the recreational facilities nearby and in the surrounding area: _____
_____
_____

19. List the daycare facilities nearby: _____
_____

20. Availability and cost of public transportation to work centers: _____
_____

21. a. Comments from discussion with VA about market in the area and the specific land: (Person contacted: _____)
_____
_____

    b. How many commitments will they give? _____

22. a. Comments from discussion with FHA about market in the area and the specific land: (Person contacted: _____)
_____
_____

    b. How many commitments will they give? _____

23. Advice from local title company: (Person and company contacted: _____)
_____
_____

24. Advice from local bank or savings & loan: (Person and company contacted: _____)
_____
_____

25. a. Are there adequate subcontractors, suppliers, and workmen in the area?
_____

    b. Union or nonunion? _____

    c. Can we use both union and nonunion? _____

26. Survey of competition:

   a. Subdivision/builder: _____

   Lot size: _____ location: _____

   Who has the advantage over location, visibility, neighborhood, etc.? _____
   _____

Plan type/garage	Sq. ft.	BR/BA/FR/etc.	Price	Number plotted	Number sold
1) _____	_____	_____	_____	_____	_____
2) _____	_____	_____	_____	_____	_____
3) _____	_____	_____	_____	_____	_____
4) _____	_____	_____	_____	_____	_____
5) _____	_____	_____	_____	_____	_____

   Total sales in _____ weeks (_____/week) . . . . . _____

   Standard features: Air-cond ☐; Tile: entry ☐ counters ☐; Rear fencing ☐; Front landscape/sprinklers ☐;

   _____ Roofs: _____; Fireplaces: _____

   Popular options and prices: _____

   Any change planned for next unit? _____

   Last price increase: _____ Increase since opening (date: _____): $_____

   Financing offered: _____

   Ad source of most buyers: _____

   How is their model presentation? _____
   _____
   _____

   b. Subdivision/builder: _____

   Lot size: _____ Location: _____

   Who has the advantage over location, visibility, neighborhood, etc.? _____
   _____

Plan type/garage	Sq. ft.	BR/BA/FR/etc.	Price	Number plotted	Number sold
1) _____	_____	_____	_____	_____	_____
2) _____	_____	_____	_____	_____	_____
3) _____	_____	_____	_____	_____	_____
4) _____	_____	_____	_____	_____	_____
5) _____	_____	_____	_____	_____	_____

Total sales in _____ weeks (_____ /week) . . . _____

Standard features: Air-cond ☐; Tile: entry ☐ counters ☐; Rear fencing ☐; Front landscape/sprinklers ☐; _____ roofs: _____; fireplaces: _____

Popular options and prices: _____

Any change planned for next unit? _____

Last price increase: _____ Increase since opening (date: _____): $_____

Financing offered: _____

Ad source of most buyers: _____

How is their model presentation? _____

c. Subdivision/builder: _____

Lot size: _____ Location: _____

Who has the advantage over location, visibility, neighborhood, etc.? _____

Plan type/garage	Sq. ft.	BR/BA/FR/etc.	Price	Number plotted	Number sold
1) _____	_____	_____	_____	_____	_____
2) _____	_____	_____	_____	_____	_____
3) _____	_____	_____	_____	_____	_____
4) _____	_____	_____	_____	_____	_____
5) _____	_____	_____	_____	_____	_____

Total sales in _____ weeks (_____ /week) . . . . . _____

Standard features: Air-cond ☐; Tile: entry ☐ counters ☐; Rear fencing ☐; Front landscape/sprinklers ☐; _____ Roofs: _____; Fireplaces: _____

Popular options and prices: _____

Any change planned for next unit? _____

Last price increase: _____ Increase since opening (date: _____): $_____

Financing offered: _____

Ad source of most buyers: _____

How is their model presentation? _____

_____

_____

   d. Subdivision/builder: _____

       Lot size: _____ Location: _____

       Who has the advantage over location, visibility, neighborhood, etc.? _____

_____

_____

Plan type/garage	Sq. ft.	BR/BA/FR/etc.	Price	Number plotted	Number sold
1) _____	_____	_____	_____	_____	_____
2) _____	_____	_____	_____	_____	_____
3) _____	_____	_____	_____	_____	_____
4) _____	_____	_____	_____	_____	_____
5) _____	_____	_____	_____	_____	_____

Total sales in _____ weeks (_____/week) . . . . . _____

_____

Standard features: Air-cond ☐; Tile: entry ☐ counters ☐; Rear fencing ☐; Front landscape/sprinklers ☐;

_____ Roofs: _____; Fireplaces: _____

Popular options and prices: _____

Any change planned for next unit? _____

Last price increase: _____ Increase since opening (date: _____): $_____

Financing offered: _____

_____

Ad source of most buyers: _____

_____

How is their model presentation? _____

_____

Additional Notes for Section 10:

11

Financial Projections

Compiled by: _____ Date: _____

	Floor Plan	Floor Plan	Floor Plan	Floor Plan	Average Per Unit	Total All Units
A. Plan description:	_____	_____	_____	_____	_____	_____
No. of units:	_____	_____	_____	_____	_____	_____
Square footage:	_____	_____	_____	_____	_____	_____
B. Prices:	$_____	$_____	$_____	$_____	$_____	$_____

C. Costs:

1. Construction costs
      per sq. ft.: $......... $......... $......... $......... $.........

   Adjusted for:

   (1) _____ .... $......... $.........
   (2) _____ .... $......... $.........
   (3) _____ .... $......... $.........

2. Adjusted construction
      cost per unit: $_____ $_____ $_____ $_____ $......... $.........

3. Cost per sq. ft.   ($_____) ($_____) ($_____) ($_____) ($_____)

4. Finished lot cost estimate:
   a. Raw lot cost $......... $.........
   b. Off-site costs per lot $......... $.........
   c. Fees per lot $_____ $_____
                              Finished lot cost: $......... $.........

5. Common area costs (describe amenities): _____ $.........

_____

55

	Average Per Unit	Total All Units

6. Indirect costs:
   a. Supervision/labor/auto/temp. facilities ($ _____ x _____ mos.): $ .... $ ....
   b. Security/plans & calcs./misc. supplies/vandalism/etc.: $_____ $_____
       (estimate based on _____)
                                     Total indirect costs: $ .... $ ....

7. Total hard costs (sum of lines 2, 4, 5, and 6): $ .... $ ....

8. Interest/property tax carry (_____ % x _____ mos. x avg.
   _____ % outstanding from construction financing): $ .... $ ....

9. Financing (construction loan points/title insurance for lender/ builder's risk insurance/points/buydowns/tax stamps/escrow/etc.)
   (_____ % of sales): $ .... $ ....

10. Commissions (_____ % of sales): $ .... $ ....

11. Merchandising (est. _____ months)
    a. Model/sales office/displays/brochures/etc. ($_____ per month): $ .... $ ....
    b. Advertising/signs/model maintenance/etc. (_____ % of sales): $_____ $_____
                                      Total merchandising costs: $ .... $ ....

12. Warranty/contingency (_____ % of sales or _____ % of costs): $ .... $ ....

13. General administration allocation (overhead allowance): $ .... $ ....

14. Total costs (sum of lines 7 through 13): $ .... $ ....

15. Profit: For-sale units (line B less line 14): $ .... $ ....
    What is profit percentage (line 15 ÷ line B)? _____ %

16. a. Is project's viability clearly indicated by this initial projection? _____
    _____

    b. If not, what can be done to make it viable (product change, site plan redesign, etc.)? _____
    _____

12

Resale

Compiled by: _____ Date: _____

1. Determine estimate of fair market value of this land:

	Per Lot	Per Acre
Raw (as purchased)	_____ =	_____
Approved specific plan or zoning	_____ =	_____
Approved tentative	_____ =	_____
Recorded map with improvement plans	_____ =	_____
Developed Lots	....	....
Less improvement cost estimate (see Development Costs)	_____	_____
Land residual	_____	_____
	_____ =	_____

2. a. To whom should we offer lots or land and why? _____
   _____

   b. What commission will we pay? _____

3. a. Which portion should we offer for sale, considering both our and buyer's access, visibility, model locations, improvement costs, etc. ? _____
   _____
   _____

   b. What easements should we retain? _____
   c. Should we retain oil and mineral rights? _____

4. a. Should we sell raw, mapped, or finished lots, and why? _____
   _____
   _____

   b. When can we deliver? _____
   c. When could buyer start construction? _____
   d. Could he or she have early access to start models? _____

5. What rights of approval should we retain? _____

6. a. On what terms should we offer land? _____

   b. What escrow deposit should be required? $ _____

   c. How long a "free look"? _____

   d. When should closing be required? _____

   e. Any basis for extension? _____

   f. Which costs should buyer bear? _____

   g. Which contingency clauses should we not allow? _____

   h. Which of buyer's contingencies should be deemed approved, after how many days? _____

7. a. What information have we discovered that we must disclose to potential buyer? _____

   b. What warranties should we give or refuse to give? _____

Additional Notes for Section 12:

13

Post-Closing Checklist

Compiled by: _____ Date: _____

1. _____ Purchase _____ Sale
2. Buyer: _____
3. Seller: _____
4. Land Description: _____
5. Closing Date: _____
6. Recorded documents inspected:
    a. Deed: _____
    b. Trust Deed: _____
       _____
    c. Other: _____
       Comments: _____
7. Settlement statement reviewed: _____
8. Receivables (Applicable _____ N/A _____):
    a. Cash received from escrow: _____
    b. Note received from escrow: _____
       Storage location: _____
       Summary of collection provisions: _____
    c. Other deferred compensation: _____
    d. Letter of Credit draw: _____
    e. Utility reimbursements: _____
    f. Other: _____
9. Payables (Applicable _____ N/A _____):
    a. Note installments: _____
    b. Letter of Credit call: _____
    c. Other: _____
10. Title policy:
    a. Date issued: _____
    b. Verification of content by Attorney: _____
                                by Engineer: _____

11. Time constraints:

   a. Obtain building permit: _____

   b. Notice to parties: _____
   _____

   c. Obtain consents or approvals: _____
   _____